Peace from Insanity

Jesse M. Arzate

Author's Tranquility Press
MARIETTA, GEORGIA

Copyright © 2022 by Jesse M. Arzate.

All rights reserved. No part of this publication may be reproduced, distributed, or transmitted in any form or by any means, including photocopying, recording, or other electronic or mechanical methods, without the prior written permission of the publisher, except in the case of brief quotations embodied in critical reviews and certain other noncommercial uses permitted by copyright law. For permission requests, write to the publisher, addressed "Attention: Permissions Coordinator," at the address below.

Jesse M. Arzate/Author's Tranquility Press
2706 Station Club Drive SW
Marietta, GA 30060
www.authorstranquilltypress.com

Ordering Information:
Quantity sales. Special discounts are available on quantity purchases by corporations, associations, and others. For details, contact the "Special Sales Department" at the address above.

Peace from Insanity: Jesse M. Arzate
Paperback: 978-1-958179-73-4
eBook: 978-1-958179-74-1

Contents

It's Seems 1
Journey 2
Woman 3
Love 4
Foundation 5
My Children 6
Loving arms 7
Art 8
Father 9
Escape 10
Gold 11
Peace 12
Chameleon 13
Friends 14
Colors 15
Eclipse 16
Mother 17
Links 18
Power 19
Harmony 20
Cotton Days 21
Winter 22
Balance 23
This world 24
Child 25

Oceans 26
Obscure 27
Never 28
Nightmare 29
Unfinished life 30
Agitators 31
Journey 32
Echo 33
Create 34
Hateful 35
Pendulum 36
Haven 37
Pillows of dreams 38
Healing 39
Trinity 40
Faith 41
Musical notes 42
Bizarre Dream 43
Reality 44
Mistakes 45
Pieces 46
Shaman 47
Revenge 48
My faith 49
This World 50
Black Rose 51
Peace from insanity 52

1
It's Seems

Sometimes it seem that the quiet
moment of life are the times
when we need to reflex
about the past
and focus on the future.

2
Journey

This journey of life
it is an interesting one.
It has its twists and turns
It's ups and downs.
It black and white
and even then
things aren't so clear.
There is love and hate
theirs are things to unite us
and things to divide us.
There is sanity and insanity
these are ingredients that
makes life an interesting journcy.

3
Woman

Woman was created
from the rib of a man
to be his companion
and not from his heel.
For a woman love is only
as giving as the love she receives.

4
Love

Love is for everyone
yet not everyone loves.

5
Foundation

Understanding compassion
and love
is the foundation
to meaningful life.

6
My Children

You're the reason I live.
You're the reason
I have joy in my heart
and meaning in my life.
And the moments
we spend together are blessings
from our love.

7
Loving arms

I wish some children's had wings
to fly away from harm.
I wish some children's had wings
to fly into loving arms.

8
Art

Love is an art by two
spending a lifetime together
creating a masterpiece of it.

9
Father

A father
far from being a mother.
Yet as important
in the role of raising a child.

Escape

I saw a child today
that took me back into a time
when life was real
yet not so true.
To a time when dreams
where more than just dreams
but a world full of adventures
where I could escape reality.

11
Gold

Looking for a mate
is like mining for gold.
Fools gold and real gold
look similar.
Yet there rewards
are very different.

12
Peace

Peace in this world
it's an unattainable dream.
Wait maybe 10 people can prove me wrong.
Maybe 10,000 people can prove me wrong.
Maybe 10 million people can prove me
wrong or more.
I would love to be proven wrong
just to see a world full of peace.

13
Chameleon

Many hearts are like chameleons
they adapt to another for the moment.
Rather than stay faithful to one forever.

14
Friends

Every friend you have
was once a stranger.
Imagine a world
without a stranger
only a world with friends.

15
Colors

It amazes how colors on a canvas
can create a masterpiece
and colors of a skin create racism.

16
Eclipse

We held each other tight
we rip each other's heart
with words.
Truth and lies eclipse
bringing darkness
Into the light.

17
Mother

She feels the miracle of life
growing inside of her.
And when the baby is born
her love becomes their bond.
For the love between mother
and child is a special love.

18
Links

May the love that link
be the love that bonds
through thick and thin.
Who is to say that love
can't prevail through life pains.

19
Power

Power and money
in the hands of some
are like matches in the hands
of an arsonist.

20
Harmony

There are so many gods and prophets.
So many worshipers
worshiping within their faiths.
Yet there so much violent,
suffering and racism.
And so many wars
with life lost.
Why do we worship
when we can't even bring
harmony and peace
into this world with our faith.

21
Cotton Days

When I was a child I walk
between rows of cotton stocks
that seem to reach the sky.
While dew rested upon the cotton
and trickle down leaves.
While the conversation between the pickers
was one full of despair that lingered in the
winter air.
For their ways of making a living had come
to an end.
It was a new beginning
humanity being replace with machinery.
Scales and trailers would be put to rest.
While the poorest were sent on their ways.
Progress has no heart or soul
as cotton pickers became a part of the past.
There's a lesson to be learned as we progress.

22
Winter

Winter days and winter nights
we can't turn back the hands of time.
Winter days and winter night
we will never stop the hands of time
from taking humanity into an uncertain future.

23
Balance

When I was a child
I had a father and a mother
the balance that gave me a life.

24
This world

From the mountains to the valley
from the ocean to the sea.
This world is too lovely
for the hatred some people
display for one another.
This world is too lovely for such ugliness.

Child

When I was a child I was told
their a God and there's a devil
that their is good and evil.
Now that I'm older
it's hard to tell them apart
as I roam within a world
of chants and prayers,
love and hate,
peace and wars.

Oceans

Their ocean between us
not those that divide lands.
But those that divide us
with powerful emotions.

27
Obscure

When I look at you
I hide within an obscure glass world.
Hard to look into
yet easy to shatter.
Anchor by my insecurity
yet when I look into your eyes
I see sincerity
while my feelings are woven
within my heart for you.

28
Never

You'll never be cuddled or loved.
You'll never grow up
and experience friendship.
You'll never see the colors
of the sunrise or sunset.
You'll never hold
a kitten or puppy in your arms.
You'll never experience falling in love.
All this and more will be denied from you
right down to your birth.

Nightmare

A white dove
falling from the sky
with a broken heart.
It landed in front of a serpent
and a saint as it died
with an olive twig in its beak.
The serpent and saint
battle over humanity
while starring into each other eyes
until they became statues to be worship upon.
Deception then fell upon
the minds and hearts of men's
who claim to have God
or prophets within their heart.
While only having the blood
of innocence lives upon their hands.
I would hate to exist in a world
with only one belief
if innocent lives are lost
because of it
it would be like living
within a nightmare.

30
Unfinished life

I was awakened within a dream
finding myself within a dark place
with white illuminating porcelain statues
with black domino mask
chanting for peace.
I heard cries from those
who had died within
the darkness of violence
as their innocent blood
fell from sky like raindrops
creating puddles of
unfinished life.

Agitators

The news agitators
surgically remove the truth
while reporting their agenda for the day.
The names are different
as the location
yet the stories remain the same.
They walk thru the protesters
salivating over the destruction of chaos.
They report disaster
one never ending rerun
they call the news.

Journey

I walk among soul
without heart and eyes without sight.
Now this is a journey
of the afterlife
where nothing exist.
Where in heaven or hell
no mortals spirit dwells.
For the kingdom of heaven
and hell
are guarded very well.

33
Echo

He sounded like an echo
without a voice.
He spoke about a nightmare
not found within a dream
but within himself.
He roamed the street of life
aimlessly with no destination.
He spoke about the war in the east
where he served far from the west.
Trying to make sense of nonsense
riddles of humanities and their wars.

34
Create

If I could create a god to worship
like those before me.
My God he will not be in
heaven looking down on us,
enjoying the perverted sadistic sitcom
humanity become.
If I could created a god to worship
like those before me
I'd wouldn't.

Hateful

We are not born hateful
we are born innocent with love.
Yet some are taught
to hate others for their skin color.
Some of us are not taught
to love others for who they are.
Some of us are not taught to love.
Some of us are just taught to hate
for whatever reason
as innocent lives are lost.

36
Pendulum

There are those who want
everything within their own power
only to take control
with their insanity.
While life becomes like a pendulum
swinging between insanity and sanity.

37
Haven

I see people sacrificing themselves
putting together their life's
like pieces of puzzle.
Creating a haven
without true happiness.

Pillows of dreams

Daffodils and lemon drops
children dreams and rain drops
nursery rhymes and lullabies
riddles and giggles
fantasies and daydreams
let's keep that part of our
childhood alive as we grow old.
For without childish imagination
life is just a blank canvas
without colorful dreams.

39
Healing

What humanity need
is a lot of healing
for their to be unity.

Trinity

I placed a crystal upon a mirror
to open doors between here and there.
As black candles flames
dance an exotic dance
while the letters A through Z
linger between the sun and moon
as I wonder which of this ten keys
will unlock this mystic door
so my Christian mind spiritual mind
and mystical mind can become
the true trinity of my life.

41
Faith

Faith is deceiving to
the heart.
Faith creates a false reality.

Musical notes

If humanity could be musical notes
and there's love create a musical
symphony of peace and harmony.
What a peaceful musical place
this world would be
if we all sang the same song
of peace and harmony.

43
Bizarre Dream

I once had a bizarre dream
that an hourglass of faith fell
from a pedestal within a temple of worship.
As it shatter all of the grain of sands
became like angels
with swords resembling demons.
They roam the earth taking life
for no one had the seal of salvation.
There was no rapture
for those who believed in it.
While all the corpses left behind
became feast for all the beast.
Now without humanity this world
became a lovely garden of peace.

Reality

There's no more true morals reality
in this world.
The only reality is the one
humanity creates for themselves
it's false and nauseating.

45
Mistakes

We all make mistakes at time
when it comes to the heart.
Our decision doesn't have to be
a mistake that shatters
a heart of the one we love.
Even though it is said
love prevails all
I believe love has limitations.

Pieces

If from the beginning of humanity
to the end of it.
If we were all just pieces
of a puzzle and when the puzzle is complete
what would it say about our existence on earth.

Shaman

The last shaman stood on the bank
of the river of life as it slowly dried
as innocent lives were lost
somewhere between dawn and dust.
Ancient winds gave way to a harsh
modern breeze
as clouds cried and earth sigh.
The last true shaman vanished
into a place of tranquility taking
his vision of clarity
into a haven of his own purity.

Revenge

I dream of a world of peace
and not a world of revenge.
A world where there is kindness and forgiveness.
Yet if revenge prevails without truth
it becomes a spectacle adding to the problem
rather than solving it
like a movement without sincerity.
While i dream of a world without revenges.

49
My faith

I see the future echoing the past
I'm losing my faith in humanity ever
living in peace.
I also have no faith in humanity
ever compromising with one another.
Humanity is too busy creating groups
of acceptance.
Some groups themselves according
to the color of their skin.
Other group themselves according
to the way they worship
while some group themselves according
to their political parties.
Some group themselves according
to their lifestyle.
There comes a time when will
group ourselves out of existence.

50
This World

My heart was faint
like a flickering lantern
as I walked through this dark world.
I prayed for strength and endurance
and was blessed with the
light of wisdom
to guide me through.

Black Rose

A black rose
pierced through a blanket of snow
only to blooms underneath a blood moon.

Peace from insanity

At times when I look at the sky
that separates me from heaven.
I wonder about God
while satan rules the government of this world
and dwells within some temples
of faith like an angel of light
creating battles between
truth and falsehoods.
Now I walk through ruins
left behind by the battles
of Cain and Able
and kneel down beside a corpse
with a crown of thorns
I pray for peace from insanity .

Jesse M Arzate

www.ingramcontent.com/pod-product-compliance
Lightning Source LLC
LaVergne TN
LVHW020439080526
838202LV00055B/5267